After Prayer

After Prayer

New sonnets and other poems

Malcolm Guite

CANTERBURY
PRESS

Norwich

© Malcolm Guite 2019

First published in 2019 by the Canterbury Press Norwich
Editorial office
3rd Floor, Invicta House
108–114 Golden Lane
London EC1Y OTG, UK
www.canterburypress.co.uk

Second impression 2020
Canterbury Press is an imprint of Hymns Ancient & Modern Ltd
(a registered charity)

H
Y Ancient
M &Modern;
N
S

Hymns Ancient & Modern® is a registered trademark of Hymns
Ancient & Modern Ltd
13A Hellesdon Park Road, Norwich,
Norfolk NR6 5DR, UK

British Library Cataloguing in Publication data

A catalogue record for this book is available
from the British Library

978 1-78622-210-7

Typeset by Regent Typesetting
Printed and bound in Great Britain by
CPI Group (UK) Ltd

For Maggie

Contents

Preface

The title sequence of this collection was begun on a retreat in
May of 2018 and completed in January of 2019. I had been
reading Herbert's beautiful little poem 'Prayer' for over 30
years, still finding new depths and new insights as, over the
years, the little seeds of his 27 astonishing images and emblems
of prayer took root and grew in my mind. I published a brief
interpretation of the poem in my book *Faith, Hope and Poetry*
in 2010, and in the last decade I have been leading retreats and
quiet days drawing on 'Prayer' as a template and a compendium
of emblems for exploring what prayer is and for discerning
where we are and where we might be going in our own prayer
lives. I had sometimes suggested to retreatants that any one
of the images in this poem might be seen as the seed, kernel,
or starting point for a new poem, and then finally, on retreat
myself, I thought I had better follow my own dictum and see
what would happen if I were to write a poem in response to
each of Herbert's seminal images.

I learnt many things by doing this, but perhaps the most telling
was the discovery that 'Prayer' is not a random compendium,
but rather a soul-story, a spiritual journey. Usually the images
flash by us so fast in such dazzling array that we have scarcely
time to consider their order, their narrative arc. But by slowing
the poem down and reflecting on each image both in itself and
in its place in the sequence I found myself taken on a journey
from the feasting and fecundity of the opening image, through
mystery and variety and then, with *the Christian plummet*,
down into unsounded depths and uncharted waters, into the
painful battle fields and the wounded places of *engine against
the almightie, sinners tower, Christ-side-piercing spear*, and

then eventually up again through a kind of chastened recovery, a training of the ear to hear new music, *a kind of tune*, until one glimpsed *the bird of paradise* and caught the scent of *the land of spices*, until one was brought at last to the brink of *something understood*. The journey, I soon realized, was not just Herbert's but had, necessarily, to be mine as well. And I found that, paradoxically, by following Herbert's trajectory so closely I was also enabled to recognize and tell something of my own story too.

The sequence is called 'After *Prayer*' both because it is written 'after' or in response to Herbert's poem and also because it is about the search for prayer, being 'after' prayer in that sense. It also records the experiences and reflections that follow on from and come after one's attempts at prayer. So I hope the sequence can be read both as a collection of individual reflections that might illuminate or converse with the reader's experience but also as a single work of 27 stanzas, a partly confessional prayer journey and journal.

I have extended the title *After Prayer* to cover the rest of this collection, as well as its opening sequence, in the hope that these other poems may also be considered as being 'after prayer' in the different senses I have outlined above. I included 'Motes', 'Amen' and the 'Seven Heavens, Seven Hells' sequence in Part I, along with 'After *Prayer*' itself, as they seemed to belong together. The 'Seven Heavens, Seven Hells' sequence of roundels was written to accompany a suite of music called *Music of the Spheres* composed by Marty O'Donnel, originally as part of the soundtrack of a video game called *Destiny* but also as a stand-alone sequence. My response was to the music, rather than to the game. The composer and I had both, in our turn, been inspired by Michael Ward's ground-breaking book *Planet Narnia*, in which he elucidated the way C. S. Lewis had quietly patterned his seven Narnia Chronicles on the seven Heavens of mediaeval astronomy, as laid out in Dante's *Paradiso*. Ward is particularly good at showing how the character of each of the spheres or planets, the Mercurial, or Martial, or Jovial character, the Solar and Lunar clusters of ideas and associations, each have a positive virtue or excellence, each an aspect of the goodness of the Logos, but each can be perverted, each is susceptible to its own particular vices, when the Jovial becomes tyrannical, the Martial bloodthirsty, the Mercurial mendacious. I used a pair of roundels for each sphere and in each pair there is a common, repeated phrase, which can be heavenly or hellish depending on its tone and intention.

The poems in Part II of this collection are more general and wide ranging, but like 'After *Prayer*' they do follow a certain pattern and path. After some opening pieces reflecting on the art of writing itself, I move through a series that reflects on the patterns and moments of faith and doubt as they impinge on our ordinary lives, together with some more open and speculative poems. My 'Rondeau for Leonard Cohen', written in response to his death and to all his music has meant to me, ushers in some of my own darker reflections on themes of loss and separation which in turn lead to a number of elegiac, commemorative, and dedicatory pieces.

'The Last Waltz' was written for the funeral of Pete Boursnell, brother of the bass player in my band who shared with us a love of the film *The Last Waltz* and of all the music and musicians featured in that film. He also founded a charity that encouraged disadvantaged young people to aim for the best universities, and both the film and his life's work are alluded to in that poem. The two sonnets for Ed and Wendy Peterson's golden wedding anniversary celebrate a Canadian couple who united in their lives and ancestry both the First Nations of Canada and the later European arrivals: Wendy counts the Red River Metis people among her ancestors and worked for an organization called Indigenous Pathways. Again, some of this background finds its way into the poems.

I also offer seven of the poems I was commissioned to write by the artist Bruce Herman as part of a project called *Ordinary Saints*. The purpose of that project, which consisted of portraits by Bruce Herman, poems of mine, and music composed by J. A. C. Redford, was to meditate on the hidden image of God in each of us, to consider what it was to look through a glass darkly, but also what it might mean to be 'face to face', with one another and with God, to see how far our human encounters might become sacraments of grace. The poems therefore turned and returned, in both rhyme and meditation, to the meetings of the words 'face' and 'grace'. There were 21 poems in the full sequence, each corresponding to a different portrait, but I have included here those poems that I thought might stand alone without their accompanying paintings, though those who would like to see the paintings themselves can find them on https://ordinary-saints.com.

There are some dark turns on the journey of this second part of *After Prayer*, some more personal equivalents of *the Christian plummet*, but as with Herbert's original poem, I do not end there, but choose rather to end with blessing and benediction.

Acknowledgements

Some of these poems first appeared in *The Church Times*, *Christian Century*, *The Plough Quarterly*, and *Spiritus*, and I am grateful to the editors of these journals for permission to collect them here.

'Strange Surprise' and 'St Augustine and the Reapers' were commissioned by Jeremy Begbie for his book *Redeeming Transcendence in the Arts* (SCM, 2019) and I am grateful for permission to include them here.

The sequence of roundels 'Seven Heavens, Seven Hells' was originally commissioned by Bungie Inc. to accompany the music composed by Marty O'Donnel, for their game *Destiny*, and the copyright rests with them. The poems are published here with their permission.

'O Virgo Virginum' was commissioned by the Precentor of Wells Cathedral for an Advent service, and forms an eighth antiphon sonnet to go with the seven in *Sounding the Seasons*.

The 'Seven Poems from *Ordinary Saints*' first appeared in *Ordinary Saints* by Bruce Herman, Malcolm Guite and J. A. C. Redford (Gloucester, Massachusetts, 2018), and are part of a sequence of ekphrastic poetry commissioned by Bruce Herman to accompany the portraits in his *Ordinary Saints* project (https://ordinary-saints.com). I am grateful for Bruce's permission to include those poems here.

'The Seasons' Benedictions' was originally commissioned by Lancia Smith for her excellent online journal *Cultivating* (https://thecultivatingproject.com) and I am glad, with her permission, to conclude *After Prayer* with these blessings.

I am grateful to Susanna Clarke, Grevel Lindop and Christopher Hodgkins for their close reading and comments on the 'After *Prayer*' sequence, and to Niki Lambros for her advice on punctuation and other matters. I am deeply indebted to Michael Ward for his reading of the whole manuscript of this book and for his helpful suggestions about the best way of ordering and sequencing these poems. I have followed his good advice to the letter.

Philippa Pearson, my PA, has worked tirelessly to lift burdens of administration from me, especially in my travels, which has left me room to write, and I am thankful, as ever, for her help.

Some of these poems were written for sessions of the Girton College Poetry Group *Not Averse*, and I am grateful to members of that group for their encouragement, comments, and criticism, and also to the Fellows, Students, and Staff of Girton College for tolerating, and indeed encouraging their chaplain's other life as a poet.

Finally, I am grateful to Christine Smith, my editor at Canterbury Press, for her constant encouragement to me as a poet, and to my wife Maggie, to whom this book is dedicated, for the love and kindness that makes my life as a writer possible.

PART I

After *Prayer*: A Response to George Herbert

Prayer George Herbert

PRAYER the Churches banquet, Angels age,
  Gods breath in man returning to his birth,
  The soul in paraphrase, heart in pilgrimage,
The Christian plummet sounding heav'n and earth;
Engine against th' Almightie, sinners towre,
  Reversed thunder, Christ-side-piercing spear,
  The six-daies-world-transposing in an houre,
A kinde of tune, which all things heare and fear;
Softnesse, and peace, and joy, and love, and blisse,
  Exalted Manna, gladnesse of the best,
  Heaven in ordinarie, man well drest,
The milkie way, the bird of Paradise,
  Church-bels beyond the starres heard, the souls blood,
  The land of spices; something understood.

1 The Church's Banquet

Not some strict modicum, exact allowance,
Precise prescription, rigid regimen,
But beauty and gratuitous abundance,
Capacious grace, beyond comparison.
Not something hasty, always snatched alone;
Junkets of junk food, fuelling our dis-ease,
Not little snacklets eaten on the run,
But peace and plenty, taken at our ease.
Not to be worked for, not another task,
But love that's lavished on us, full and free,
Course after course of hospitality,
And rich wine flowing from an unstopped flask.
He paid the price before we reached the inn,
And all he asks of us is to begin.

2 Angel's Age

How might my prayer partake the *angels' age*?
Theirs is no age at all, but all in one;
My moments pass, as steps in pilgrimage,
But they begin where my dark journey's done.
They see all things at once: each point in time
For them is radiant with eternity.
Mine are the twists and turns, the long road home,
Theirs is the over-view, and flying free
They brush me with their feathers, with the rumour
Of their flight, and something in me sings
Into their passing light, till my prayer-murmur,
Circled in the slipstream of their wings,
Is lifted up in grace to join with theirs,
Who sing a *Sanctus* into all our prayers.

3 God's Breath in Man Returning to his Birth

Breathe in and in that breathing be created,
Wake from the dust, be conscious and inhale
Fresh from the Word and Light of God, delighted,
You find you have become a living soul.
But soon you must breathe out. What's to be done?
Who will be with you then? And will you dare
To trust the breath of life back to the one
Who breathed it into you? Christ comes to share
Your letting go; you hear him sigh and say
Father into your hands receive my spirit
And find that he has opened up the way
For you as well. He takes your breath to bear it
Deep into heaven with him in his death,
That you might be reborn with every breath.

4 The Soul in Paraphrase

A fledgling hidden in an ancient tree,
Singing unseen and darkling to the stars,
The fount and spring of meaning, just upstream
Of every utterance, unsullied, free,
A prisoner who grips and bends her bars,
The one who begs to differ, dares to dream,
A child astray, still calling to your heart,
A pattern, personal as all the swirls
In fingerprints on hands that hands have held,
Wholeness that knows itself within each part,
A flag whose emblem every breath unfurls,
A chasm bridged, and an old heartache healed,
A new day at the end of all your days,
A mystery you'll never paraphrase.

5 Heart in Pilgrimage

I start with Dante in a darkened wood
Well past the middle of my mazy way,
My beating heart sustains this flesh and blood,

A sounding drum that will not let me stay
Stuck in the sluggishness of middle age.
For here are April showers and a new day,

As Chaucer joins me in my pilgrimage;
The mottled glory of his company,
With all their tales to tell, gives me new courage.

And now a Bedford tinker comes to me
And sings: *Here little, and hereafter bliss,*
Death where's thy sting, where grave thy victory?

So, pilgrim heart, keep beating, fierce and free,
Your last beat brings me where I long to be.

6 The Christian Plummet

Down into the icy depths you plunge,
The cold dark undertow of your depression,
Even your memories of light made strange,
As you fall further from all comprehension.
You feel as though they've thrown you overboard,
Your fellow Christians on the sunlit deck,
A stone-cold Jonah on whom scorn is poured,
A sacrifice to save them from the wreck.

But someone has their hands on your long line,
You sound for them the depths they sail above,
One who takes Jonah as his only sign
Sinks lower still to hold you in his love,
And though you cannot see, or speak, or breathe,
The everlasting arms are underneath.

7 Engine Against Th' Almightie

Here in this shadowed valley, dark and bleak,
We lay a bitter siege against the one
Who was our heart's desire, but now withdraws
Behind his battlements. Our prayers just break
Against what seem like walls of silent stone.
We make an engine of our injuries,
And vault at God a volley of our sorrows:
All the despair and anger that we feel.
The catapult of our catastrophes
Hurls up its heavy load, and flights of arrows
Clatter against his walls, fall back and fail.
How can we make him feel our miseries?
We fling back famine at him, torture, cancer,
Is he almighty then? Has he no answer?

8 Sinner's Tower

Exhausted by my own siege engine's roar,
The clatter and the rattle of my prayer,
I drop, defeated, at his bolted door,
And sink awhile in silence and despair.
Is there another way to come at him,
Who seems so distant in his might and power?
I have no wings to rise like seraphim
So I begin to build the sinner's tower,
Returning to that folly back in Babel.
Effort and elevation are my aim,
As though by my own powers I were able
To overwrite the nameless with my name.
But just before the summit and the crown
A voice in darkness calls: 'let us go down'.

9 Reversèd Thunder

This light is muffled, muted, murky, dense,
Thick with a threat of thunder unreleased.
The clouds are darkening, the air grows tense,
The coming storm is lowering in the east.
Something within me trembles too, and pales,
Though no one sees the brooding darkness there,
Or feels the tension building between poles
Of faith and doubt, of vision and despair.

Everything deepens, gathers to a head:
Anguish and anger at my absent God
Until the charge of all that's left unsaid
Leaps out at last to find its lightening rod.
But even as the skies are rent and riven
I find that lightening rod is earthed in heaven.

10 Christ's Side-piercing Spear

For all the while I hurl my hurts at heaven,
Believing I besiege the battlement
Of God's invulnerable heart and haven,
I strike at emptiness, at my own bafflement,
I shake my fist in fury at a shadow.
For he is not like us nor are his ways
Like ours. He left that heaven's haven long ago
And broke our siege. A voice behind me says:

Why do you weep and rage at heaven above?
I have come down to die here in the dirt,
Your wounds have wounded me, for I am Love
And in my heart I hold your deepest hurt.
Oh turn around, return, and face me here
Your slightest prayer will pierce me like a spear.

11 The Six Days World Transposing in an Hour

Twenty-four seven in 'the six days world',
In endless cycles of unnerving news,
Relentlessly our restless hurts are hurled
Through empty cyber-space. Is there no muse
To make of all that pain an elegy,
Or in those waves of white noise to discern
Christ's inner *cantus firmus*, that deep tone
That might give rise at last to harmony?

We may not seal it off or drown it out,
Nor close our hearts down in the hour of prayer,
But listening through dissonance and doubt,
Wait in the space between, until we hear
A change of key, a secret chord disclosed,
A kind of tune, and all the world transposed.

12 A Kind of Tune

A kind of tune, a music everywhere
And nowhere. Love's long lovely undersong,
A trace in time, a grace-note in the air,
Borne to us from the place where we belong
On every passing breeze and in the breath
Of every creature. *All things hear and fear*,
For faintly, through our fall, we too may hear
The strong song of the Son that undoes death.

And one day we will hear it unimpaired:
The joy of all the sorrowful, the song
Of all the saints who cry 'how long',
The hidden hope of all who have despaired.
He sang it to his mother in the womb
And now it echoes from his empty tomb.

13 Softness

Softness and peace and joy and love and bliss,
They rise like steps ascending to his throne,
Each step a blessing and a power to bless,
A strength in knowing and in being known
In Christ's strong love. *Softness* is first: a grace
That sets aside our strife, undoes our stress,
As hard lines soften in a kindly face
And hard toil softens into real rest,
As when, on days all strewn with broken glass,
Days we have borne with bleakness all alone,
We turn at last to take the hard road home
And someone greets us with a soft caress,
Brushing away the tears that blind our sight,
Soothing the down of darkness into light.

14 Peace

Not as the world gives, not the victor's peace,
Not to be fought for, hard-won, or achieved,
Just grace and mercy, gratefully received:
An undeserved and unforeseen release,
As the cold chains of memory and wrath
Fall from our hearts before we are aware,
Their rusty locks all picked by patient prayer,
Till closed doors open, and we see a path
Descending from a source we cannot see;
A path that must be taken, hand in hand,
Only by those, forgiving and forgiven,
Who see their saviour in their enemy.
So reach for me. We'll cross our broken land,
And make each other bridges back to heaven.

15 Joy

How does she come, my joy, when she comes walking
Over the wasteland and the empty waves?
She comes unbidden between sleep and waking,
She comes like winter jasmine on cold graves,
She comes like some swift wind, she fills my sails,
And on we surge, cresting the wine-dark sea,
The fine prow lifting, as my vessel heels,
The tiller tugs and quivers and I'm free
Of all the land's long cares. As that brisk breeze
Sings in the thrill and tremor of taut stays,
So my heart's rigging, tuned and taut as these,
Sings with the wind that freshens into praise.
For when Joy comes, however brief her stay,
She parts my lips and I know how to pray.

16 Love

Love took George Herbert's hand and now takes mine,
The same quick eyes, the same wry, welcome smile,
The same spear-pierced and always-healing heart.
He turns to me and taking bread and wine,
He spreads a table in the desert, while
I hesitate and draw back, stand apart,
Afraid as always, of committed love.
But I have come too far to turn away,
Though Joy has vanished, she has led me here.
'So come', says Love, 'there's nothing left to prove,
And nothing that you need to do or say,
I am that perfect love that casts out fear,
Sit with George Herbert here, then taste and see
And find that all your loves are found in me.'

17 Bliss

Softness and peace and joy and love and bliss,
Love made this way, and lifts us up each stair.
Our maker knows that we were made for this
The utter bliss that heaven loves to share.
We glimpse it sometimes in another's eyes,
We taste it sometimes on the tongues of prayer
It takes us wholly, takes us by surprise,
But grasping it, our arms clasp empty air.

Our bliss has vanished with a word of promise,
A sweet come-hither wave that offers more.
Each ecstasy has been a farewell kiss
That left us weeping on the hither shore.
Yet every passing moment whispers this:
Eternity shall love us into bliss.

18 Exalted Manna

I love to lift you in the Eucharist,
For you descended to the depth for me,
You stooped beneath the whole weight of the world,
And held it as the nails drove through each wrist,
You held us all through your long agony,
Held all the taunts and curses that we hurled
Held all our hurts deep in your heart for healing.
And when we lifted you onto your cross
You lifted all of us up to the Father
And made your outspread arms a sign, revealing
God's all-sustaining love, that bears our loss,
Becomes our daily bread, calls us to gather
Each love, as manna in the wilderness.
So lift me as I lift you, lift and bless.

19 Gladness of the Best

If prayer itself is gladness of the best,
Then all the best in everything is prayer.
Everything excellent, from east to west,
The best of sacred, best of secular,
The Beatles sing *you know you should be glad*
And that glad song is gladness of the best,
You know you're loved, *you know that can't be bad*,
Your once-lost love is found and you are blessed.

From that exultant sound in Abbey Road
To jubilation in the Albert Hall,
From well-honed phrases, to a well-wrought ode,
Whatsoever things are lovely, all
Brought to the source of every excellence,
That God might give them back as sacraments.

20 Heaven in Ordinary

Because high heaven made itself so low
That I might glimpse it through a stable door,
Or hear it bless me through a hammer blow,
And call me through the voices of the poor,
Unbidden now, its hidden light breaks through
Amidst the clutter of the every day,
Illuminating things I thought I knew,
Whose dark glass brightens, even as I pray.

Then this world's walls no longer stay my eyes,
A veil is lifted likewise from my heart,
The moment holds me in its strange surprise,
The gates of paradise are drawn apart,
I see his tree, with blossom on its bough,
And nothing can be ordinary now.

21 Man Well Dressed

That old voice from the past: *I was afraid,*
For I was naked; and I hid myself.
And somehow I'm still there, lost in that glade,
Feeling exposed, ashamed, and, in my stealth
Still holding the fell fruit. He finds me as
My withered fig leaves fall away, and still
He clothes me, for the way of heaven is
Always to give and give to those who steal.

But now the skin I'm clothed in is his own,
He makes himself a garment for us all,
At once the bridegroom and the wedding gown.
I step forth from the thicket of my fall
Already dressed in every gift he gave,
Gathered and girdled in his circling love.

22 The Milky Way

It's always there, but when our lights are low,
Or altogether out, we see it shine;
Only when things are darkest here below
Do we discern its soft pearlescent sheen,
Gracefully traced across the midnight sky,
In whose light Herbert saw the path of prayer.
Though pale and milky to the naked eye,
The view from Hubble, far above the air,
Shows us a star-field rich with many colours
'Patines of bright gold' and blue and red,
Abundance of a hundred billion stars
Whose centre lies in Sagittarius,
Darting their glory, like the myriad
Of saints and angels who all pray for us.

23 The Bird of Paradise

Poor bird of paradise: she finds nowhere
To rest or settle on her long flight home,
But circles the blue heavens endlessly
Or so we once believed, and she became
A perfect emblem of unceasing prayer:
Born out of paradise and restlessly
Seeking return, pressing on steady wings,
Beating perpetual blessing through the air,
Which parts to give her passage, and still brings
Us echoes of the haunting song she sings.
I find in her a fitting emblem too,
She sings in me, but now she is the one
In Dylan's song, who keeps on keeping on,
Like all of us, still tangled up in blue.

24 Church Bells Beyond the Stars Heard

Is it our bells they hear beyond the stars,
Or theirs whose echo sounds to us below?
Or is it both? The music of the spheres
Which we imagine, and yet cannot know,
Whose ringing joy we hear and do not hear,
Elicits a response, and our church bells,
Whose steepled peals still ring in each New Year,
All cry and clamour for the time that tells
Us time itself is over, the dark veil
Is lifted, and we see the radiant face
Of Love in everything; the mournful bell
That tolled for all our funerals gives place
To heaven's music truly heard at last,
Our last change rung on earth, our last pain past.

25 The Soul's Blood

O unacknowledged, rich and living stream,
Dark river in each vein and artery,
You pulse within us, even as we dream·
Our lifeblood, our salvation's mystery,
We all ignore you till we bruise and bleed,
And you bloom red and reach the upper air,
And then we know and see you in our need
And every heartbeat is our body's prayer,

As every pulse of prayer is our soul's blood:
Some coursing through us all unconsciously,
Some owned and known and spoken out for good,
All given and returned, all flowing free
From heaven to earth and back to heaven, where
The heart of Jesus beats in every prayer.

26 The Land of Spices

The land of spices is not far away
But planted close and gathered in one place
Ready to loose its perfume as we pray
And steal into the soul with subtle grace.
My prayer is set as incense in thy sight,
So Herbert and the whole church prayed their psalm,
His Prayer Book was a garden of delight,
Of many herbs and spices, myrrh and balm,
A fountain sealed, an orchard of rare trees
Of frankincense and aloes, cinnamon,
Whose scents, all summoned by a southern breeze,
Roused him to love and loving, stirred him on.
My soul too yearns to be where it belongs:
The fragrant garden of the Song of Songs.

27 Something Understood

And so the spell of *Prayer* comes to an end,
An end that offers us a place to start,
An invitation from a loving friend,
A colloquy where 'heart speaks unto heart'.
These twenty-six attempts to say the Name,
The simple letters of prayer's alphabet,
Bring us a little way, but end the same
Just on the brink of what's not spoken yet.

With each new understanding we begin
Again, and turn from text to mystery
To prayer itself, that draws us deeper in
Where knowledge ends, but love has mastery.
Still on that brink, I share, as pilgrims should,
Some of the somethings I have understood.

Motes

In stillness after prayer
A shaft of sunlight finds my quiet room,
Where motes of dust are dancing in the air.
Pinpoints of insight, lightening the gloom,
Appear and disappear

Like little galaxies;
Dark matter offered fleetingly to sight.
And all my thoughts are little more than these,
I bless the breath that lifts them to the light,
These moving mysteries.

And each breath after prayer
Is somehow shared, is somehow more than mine,
Making my little room an everywhere,
Its ordinary clutter seems to shine
Like starlight after prayer.

Amen

When will I ever learn to say *Amen*,
Really assent at last to anything?
For now my hesitations always bring
Some reservation in their trail, and then
Each reservation brings new hesitations;
All my intended *amens* just collapse
In an evasive mumble: *well, perhaps,*
Let me consider all the implications...

But you can read my heart, I hear you say:
For once be present to me, I am here,
Breathe in the perfect love that casts out fear
Open your heart and let your yea be yea.
Oh, bring me to that brink, that moment when
I see your full-eyed love and say *Amen*.

Seven Heavens, Seven Hells:
A Sequence for the Spheres

For Michael Ward

1 The Moon

I

The moon is full and snow falls soft tonight
In silver filigree. I seem to fall,
Floating through the chapel of her light,
The moon is full.

The white lace of the snowfall makes a veil
Through which I glimpse her face, a paler white,
Whose pallor calls to me, a tidal pull

That gathers in me, loosens, lifts the weight
That palls and pulls me. In her light I feel
Fasted and lifted, empty, open, light,
The moon is full.

II

The moon is full and I have lost my way,
Drawn down her mazy path towards my fall,
Ready to swoon and sink beneath her sway.
The moon is full.

The tide of panic rises and I feel
A dark fear that deletes the light of day.
Her pale light wraps around me like a pall

That pulls and blurs and blends and wipes away
And drains the patterns from my mind, until
She empties me and I can only say
The moon is full.

2 Mercury

I

Quicksilver messenger come flying here
And bring the secret burden that you bear
Your finger to your lips, a silent seer,
Quicksilver messenger.

Fly through the light of one bright solar flare,
Carry your secret sealed within its sphere,
With every possibility encoded there.

A helix-woven-wand has brought you here
As swift as hidden waves in empty air.
Now loose the lock, and make your meaning clear,
Quicksilver messenger.

II

Quicksilver messenger your lips are sealed
With that dark secret shrouded round in fear.
Everything's shadowed, nothing is revealed
Quicksilver messenger.

No one will whisper it, no one will hear,
Doubly occluded, doubly concealed
Behind the firewall of your secret sphere

Whose codes and combinations always shield
The occult and its dark ambassador.
Your message is hermetically sealed
Quicksilver messenger.

3 Venus

I

The morning star is lucent on the hill
To bless our flesh with yearning from afar.
She shines beyond and brightens in us still
The morning star.

All her caresses, soft and tender, are
Like overflowing water at the well,
Like waves that spill themselves onto the shore.

She comes to make us fruitful, to fulfil
The deep desires we shape with her and share
With one another. With her all is well,
The morning star.

II

The morning star, the light that fell to earth,
Infernal Venus, sometime Lucifer,
Whose dark womb brings the worst in us to birth,
The morning star.

Her tender touch will always leave a scar,
The drowsy murmuration of her breath
Floats us away beyond the saving shore

And when we wake with her she drowns us both
Though even as we drown we beg for more.
All her delights deliver us to death,
The morning star.

4 The Sun

I

Bring out the gold in me, O golden sphere
Whose light and splendour none has ever told,
Alchemic archer, brilliant charioteer,
Bring out the gold.

For you were worshipped in the days of old
As bright Apollo. Shine upon me here
And penetrate with light this mortal mould.

Sphere of the poet, prophet, sage and seer,
Lighten my inner eye till truths unfold
And blindness turns to sight. Make all things clear,
Bring out the gold.

II

Bring out the gold and let the deal be done,
For everything at last is bought and sold,
The final tribulation has begun,
Bring out the gold.

Bring in the darkest forces from the cold
And make a show of all we used to shun,
For all the payrolled do as they are told,

And lust for something new under the sun,
And do not care for whom the bell is tolled.
Bring in the day when dreadful things are done,
Bring out the gold.

5 Mars

I

Rise up and stand for what you know is right,
Marshall your strength and take the upper hand,
Be braced and ready in the morning light
Rise up and stand.

The trumpet calls through the bright martial band
To rouse the brave and free with sound and sight,
The red rose kindles to a flaming brand

When Love needs her defenders. Though the night
Is long and dark, deliverance is at hand!
So, battle-hardened, fearless in the fight,
Rise up and stand.

II

Rise up and stand to grasp with iron will
The spoils of war, the conquest of the land.
Whilst there is war to wage and blood to spill
Rise up and stand.

Although the ground you gain is red and stained
The spirit of the gladiator still
Gives you the strength you need. You are sustained

To prove again that might is right, until
The cup of blood you offer to the grand
Conquistador is drained. He drinks his fill,
Rise up and stand!

6 Jupiter

I

Come fill the cup and let the fountain flow
Your king has come! There is a feast to keep
With kindled eyes and faces all aglow
Come fill the cup.

There is a joy that makes the spirit leap
And makes the humble greater than they know.
You break the bread, the wine is at your lip,

Rich music stirs your spirit, solemn, slow
Whose true nobility still draws you up
Beyond your self with blessings to bestow.
Come, fill the cup.

II

Come fill the cup, whether you will or no,
For the Great Leader, you will drink it up.
His grateful people must put on a show.
Come fill the cup

Or you and yours will suffer. One false step
And someone disappears. They say below
His banquet hall the tortured cry for help

But Death, delaying, comes to them too slow.
So you must march and cheer and make things up.
That you may drown the truth you should not know
Come, fill the cup.

7 Saturn

I

In every heart-break wisdom can be found,
The end of things may be the place to start,
The hard frost helps to break the stony ground
In every heart.

Nothing remains the same, things fall apart.
We listen for the music; not a sound.
But we discover, silent and apart,

As meditative minutes circle round,
There is a deeper dance, an inner art,
There is a hidden treasure to be found
In every heart.

II

In every heartbreak he is to be found.
He is the end. He makes things fall apart.
There is a prison where his slaves are bound
In every heart.

He crushes hope before we even start
His prisoners must tread the dreary round
Of repetition, lonely and apart.

In him there is no mercy to be found,
No truth, no grace, no beauty and no art,
Only the grave, the cold and stony ground
In every heart.

PART II

Lost and Found

Shed-Fever

I must go down to the shed again
The lonely shed and the den
And all I ask is a kindly muse
And a hand to guide my pen,
And the verse-kick, and the vowel-song
And words warm and willing,
And a quiet time, and a full rhyme
And the white page filling.

Preliminary Ritual

First there is the clearing of the desk,
Displacing chaos for a working space,
And then the putting of each thing in place:
The pen and paper, ready for the task.
And then there is the opening of the pen,
The lifting of its lovely silver cap,
Which fits back on the barrel with a snap
Leaving the golden nib exposed. And then
With pen in hand you try a line or two
On scrap paper, you have a little go
To test how well both thought and ink might flow,
Hoping to find that both are coming through.
And so they are, but both are poor and thin,
Will they be turned aside by this harsh age?
Your pen is poised above the empty page
There's nothing for it now, but to begin.

Emily Dickinson's Desk

So slight and spare a square of wood
Sustains so great a muse –
How plain and flat the entrance is
To such a subtle maze

Perhaps the limits of this desk –
Its strict restraint of space –
Informed the poet's take and task
And turned restraint to grace

Here in this narrow paradise
She pledged and kept her troth –
And trimmed her lamp and trained her verse –
And – slant-wise – told her truth.

17 Gough Square

I find his door and climb the footworn stair
Up from the ground-floor bookshop and displays,
Past the old sitting room and parlour, where
He met the world and fended off its praise,
Up to his long-benched attic where the maze
Of language opened up and swallowed him,
Even as he mapped, in vain, the alley-ways,
The back-street derivations; every name
The entrance to some court or dwelling place
In the city of signs, each word an open door
Into another city. There he'd face
His failure, find that words are always more
Than any definition. They prefer
The City to the lexicographer.

Dactylics

Pushing away from iambic pentameters,
Stressing instead the first beat of each bar,
Dactyls can change your poetic parameters
Challenge your sense of the poet you are.

What if they open a casket locked fast in you,
Dredge up a treasure from under the wave?
What if the pattern connects with the past in you?
What if it raises a voice from the grave?

What if these dactyls are bringing a word to you,
Teaching you knowledge you'd rather refuse?
Telling you something that once seemed absurd to you:
'Mortal immortal, to win you must lose!

Let go your craving for unchecked continuance,
Weary existence with nothing to say,
Better to die than continue in ignorance,
Only through darkness you rise to the day.'

A Little Contraband

They stopped and turned my body at the border,
Denied me entry, kept me from my friends,
But there are truths that countermand their order,
'There's a divinity that shapes our ends'.
For even as I'm turned back and restricted,
My thoughts are flying free across the line,
Careless of any penalties inflicted,
My poetry makes free of all that's mine.
They held the guns but I held all the cards,
The Jack of Hearts was on my saviour's sleeve,
They were too late to stop this flow of words,
And poetry stole past without their leave.
This sonnet stands for me, right where you stand
My gift to you – a little contraband.

Revisions

He thought he had his final lines perfected,
A hesitant goodbye to her, they read:
It seems you only saw me when reflected
In the dark glass of our passion, when instead
I saw you only on the morning after,
As though, however close we came, we missed
Each other somehow. All our tears and laughter
Were in vain. Goodbye. I'm glad we kissed.

No good. He tried again. New lines, inflected
With elegiac undertones, they read:
Like empty arches in the lake reflected,
Like echoes in the reedy river bed,
Like whispers in the dark, and hollow laughter,
Like once-familiar landmarks in the mist,
Our love has faded from us, and hereafter
Only the dead will ever know we kissed.

It wouldn't do. One last attempt, perfected,
Crafted for total clarity, now read:
I've thought about this long and hard, reflected
On everything we've felt and done and said
And none of it can reach me. Maybe laughter
Will revisit you, but a cold mist
Dissolves me now into the dark hereafter...
She called, he laid his pen down, and they kissed.

How to Scan a Poet

My doctor tells me I will need a scan;
I tap a nervous rhythm with my feet,
'Just count to five,' she says, 'and then sit down

The gist of it is printed on this sheet,
So read it over when you are at home.
We'll have a clearer picture when we meet.'

I read the letter in a waiting room,
It's language strangely rich for one like me:
Image, Contrast, Resonance; a poem

Slips into view amidst the litany
Of Latin terms that make our medicine
A new poetic terminology.

The door is opened. I am ushered in
To lisp my list of symptoms, to rehearse
The undiscovered art of naming pain.

'It's called *deep inspiration*,' says the nurse,
'Draw deep for me then simply hold your breath
And stay composed.' So I compose this verse.

She says 'We dye for contrast, to unearth
Each hidden image, which might bring
Some clue that takes us closer to the truth.

Be still and I will pass you through the ring,
Three passes, all in rhythm, and you're free,
The resonance will show us everything.'

And now my Muse says much the same to me,
Scanning these lines, and calling me to sing.

Photo-graphy

Light-writing? Well there's nothing left to write,
The camera must supersede the ode,
And every subtle shimmer of the light
Be rendered and reduced to so much code:
On-off, on-off, on-off. The noughts and ones
Add up to nothing you can comprehend,
A print-out, like the print-out of old bones,
A genome iteration without end.

We cannot code or decode our own baggage,
A cut too subtle for our subtle knife,
So I cut free from my downloaded image,
To seek again the analogues of life,
The mysteries we screen off with this screen.
I go off-screen to see and to be seen.

Half-life, *an epitaph*

The life he left,
He skipped and skyped,
Half-hyphenated
Hyphen-hyped:
No book but face-
No space but my-
No tune but i-
No mail but e-
No roots, no tree
No he nor she
With love to share,
To bind and bear ...

Death did not digitise
His unrecorded cries
His last unsampled sighs.
Deleted without trace,
In placeless cyber-space,
He lived no second-life.

On some enduring stone let this be carved,
Life hyphen-hyped is only hyphen-halved.

Lost and Found

For Robert Macfarlane

Slip past the scanners and creep in between
The wireless meshes of tenacious networks.
Stay with the mystery, remain unseen,
Unfindable behind these shadowed earthworks.
Wait till the waves are gone, the way is clear,
The one location, always unlocated,
The last of earth, is always somewhere near.
Time out of time, uncounted and undated,
Awaits you there, but you must come unknown
Through your own shadow, crouched and hushed
   and deathly.
You lose the light, and find yourself alone,
Feeling your way beyond the only path
Through that dark wood, until you catch your breath
And your lost heart is earthed to the unearthly.

Questions for a Painting by Giovanni Bellini

Beyond a lintel of cold marble, breathing,
Who are these figures on the other side,
Their golden flesh emerging from the dark?

Ages and stages of our passing life,
Con-centred on the mystery of birth?

The Virgin, the Wise-Woman, Mother, Father,
Lover, Brother, Magus, gathered here
And a little child to lead them ...
Or is this Child the parent of them all?

Once-woven in the womb, now wrapped in bands,
White linen for the grave, linen for swaddling,
Through which our holy flesh already shines ...

Does she receive him from the hands of Wisdom,
Or pass him softly to the hands of Death?

O Virgo Virginum

O Virgo virginum, quomodo fiet istud?
Quia nec primam similem visa es nec habere sequentem.
Filiae Jerusalem, quid me admiramini?
Divinum est mysterium hoc quod cernitis.

O Virgin of virgins, how shall this be?
For neither before thee was any like thee, nor shall there
*   be after.*
Daughters of Jerusalem, why marvel ye at me?
The thing which ye behold is a divine mystery.

Who are the daughters of Jerusalem,
Who glimpse you still as you transform their seeing?
Whom have you called to this *mysterium*,
And bathed in the blithe fountain of your being?
Daughters of sorrow, daughters of despair,
The cast-aside, the overlooked, the spurned
The broken girls who scarcely breathe a prayer
The ones whose love has never been returned.

O Maid amongst the maidens, turn your face,
For when we glimpse you we are not alone,
O look us out of grief and into grace,
Lift us in love made stronger than our own,
Summon the spring in our worst wilderness,
And make us fruitful in your fruitfulness.

First Christmas

I, like an usurpt towne, to'another due,
Labour to'admit you, but Oh, to no end
Donne

Once only – yes – it hasn't happened yet,
And if it does, can only happen once.
For now he keeps the bounds that we have set,
We will not let him break through our defence ...
I gaze across the world at Bethlehem;
Her ruined olive trees and raided grain.
The 'house of bread' is broken once again;
Even the shepherds' fields denied to them,
Check-points and road-blocks round an usurpt town,
Every device for keeping Love at bay.
The soldiers laugh (as angels hold their breath),
They sneer at Mary's papers, turn her down.
She's on the long trek back to Nazareth,

Lest we should wake to our first Christmas Day.

The Song of the Hart

Quemadmodum desiderat cervus ad fontes aquarum,
Ita desiderat anima mea ad te, Deus.
Psalm 42.1

Our memory is also his creation.
Finding an antler in the bric-a-brac,
I run my hand along its corrugations
And imagine the living deer
Deep in the forests of Eire.

And when I lift it I hear the monk's bell.
Stirring with the figures in an old fable
Is Colm's disciple,
Out in every weather,
Blessing each creature
In his church Latin,
Who watches at matins
The careful spider
Spin a frail web
Beneath the dark heather.

He is blessing the flesh he denies
As his bones freeze to the marrow;
Glimpsed in the otter's sharp eyes,
Gathering watercress
'In a place without sorrow',
Who hears the heath-hen calling to her mate
And keeps his winter vigil with the wolves
Who call upon God for their meat.

The hermit has faded into the wilderness,
The stag's fixed antlers are dismantled.
Amidst green-fronded ferns
In a white mist
The hunter stands terrified
As his quarry turns:
For he is facing Christ recrucified
Between the spreading antlers.

This is all that remains
As speech after breath is released
And breath still mists the glass
That's freezing in these window-panes.
Beyond those windows in the mist
He feels for his footing on a hill
In soft rain seeking his rest
While the spent bullet works its way
Through a broken web of veins.
Before the sun rose he fell,
His antlers grazed the wet grass,
His head turned to the east.

His creation is also our memory
Who gave such delicate creatures breath,
Who gave them his intricate forests to walk in,
Who will not forsake us, but grants us again
The fullness of his Mystery:
Suffering, passion and death.

Aubade

And are you sleeping still my love?
The sun is on the rise,
A gentle west wind lifts the leaves,
And songbirds fill the skies.

I closed my eyes in sorrow love,
My heart as cold as stone,
And thought, as darkness covered me,
That I would lie alone.

I closed my eyes in weariness,
I closed my eyes in pain,
And never thought I should be called
To open them again.

But you were not alone my love,
Your weariness was mine,
I brought a light into the dark
That you might see it shine.

I too endured the deadly cold
That chilled us to the bone,
That I might warm the sepulchre
And roll away the stone.

Awaken now to life my love,
Arise alive and free,
Shake off the sleep of death my love,
And come away with me.

And she has risen from her bed
And held her arms out wide
And touched his wounded hands and heart
And gone to be his bride.

A Villanelle on Easter Day

As though some heavy stone were rolled away,
You find an open door where all was closed,
Wide as an empty tomb on Easter Day.

Lost in your own dark wood, alone, astray,
You pause, as though some secret were disclosed,
As though some heavy stone were rolled away.

You glimpse the sky above you, wan and grey,
Wide through those shadowed branches interposed,
Wide as an empty tomb on Easter Day.

Perhaps there's light enough to find your way,
For now the tangled wood feels less enclosed,
As though some heavy stone were rolled away.

You lift your feet out of the miry clay
And seek the light in which you once reposed,
Wide as an empty tomb on Easter Day.

And then Love calls your name, you hear him say:
The way is open, death has been deposed,
As though some heavy stone were rolled away,
And you are free at last on Easter Day.

A Lens

That All, which always is all everywhere ...
Donne

Not that we think he is confined to us,
Locked in the box of our religious rites,
Or curtained by these frail cathedral walls,
No church is broad or creed compendious
Enough. All thought's a narrowing of sites,
Before him every definition fails,
Words fall and flutter into emptiness,
Like motes of dust within his spaciousness.

Not that we summon him, but that he lends
The very means whereby he might be known,
Till this opacity of stone on stone,
This trace of light and music on the air,
This sacred space itself becomes a lens
To sense his presence who is everywhere.

Strange Surprise

None of this need have happened, all of this,
These unexpected gifts, this overflow
Of things we know, and things we'll never know,
None of this had to be, but here it is,
The here-and-now in all its strange surprise;
A space to be ourselves in, and a grace
That spins us round and turns us to the source
Whence all these gifts and graces still arise.

And now the one through whom all this was made,
Whom we ignore, on whom we turn our back,
Whom we denied, insulted and betrayed,
Gathers and offers for us all we lack,
Voices on our behalf creation's praise,
And calls us to become the song he plays.

Iona Song

Let meadows and let meadows, sea-green meadows
Lift from the waves that I am dreaming of.
Let shallows and let shallows, sun-lit shallows
Lap in the sunlight all my sea-shore love.
Let shadows and let shadows, fearful shadows
Leap from the light they dart and swoop above,
And dart through all my sorrows' sorrows' sorrows
Your sharp, delightful, fire-feathered dove.

St Francis Drops in on My Gig

I didn't think I'd find you in this place,
I guess you must have slipped in at the back,
I'm lifting my guitar out of its case,
But seeing you I nearly put it back!
You smile and say that it's your local too,
You know the ins and outs of inns like this,
The people here have hidden wounds like you,
And you have bidden them to hidden bliss.

Francis I've only straggled after you,
I've never really caught your melody,
The joy you bring when every note rings true.
But you just laugh and say 'play one for me!'
This one's for you then, on the road once more,
The first, the last, the hard-core troubadour.

St Augustine and the Reapers

What else can you do but jubilate?
St Augustine, *On the Psalms*

Augustine hears the sound of jubilation,
A snatch of song, hurrahing in the harvest,
He pauses, poised and open, pen in hand,
Held in the gracious space between God's words,
And once again his restless heart is lifted
Within and through the song, into the Son.

A wordless song restores to him the words
Of scripture and his psalter breathes again.
'Not circumscribed by syllables', but still
Delighting in them, jubilant, his pen
Turns to the furrow, opens the good ground,
So that the seed a psalmist sowed in tears
Might bear rich fruit for us in time to come.
We reap with joy and bring the harvest home.

Four Voices

I am the Salamander and I shimmer in the fire
I thrive within a living flame, desiring to desire,
I burn away the dross in you, and teach you to aspire
I am your Salamander if you'll kindle me a fire.

I am the Sylph who loved you once, a creature of the air,
I whisper just behind you but you never find me there.
I am the one you stifle when you give in to despair,
But I could breathe you back to life if you would give me air.

I am the dying Naiad in your long-neglected well,
I sing the very springs of love whose flow you fear and quell,
The sacred river rises here, if you will say the spell,
And listen for my weeping as it echoes from your well.

I am the sleeping Adam whom you buried in the earth
But give me fire, air, and rain, and I will give you birth.

A Rondeau for Leonard Cohen

Like David's psalm you named our pain,
And left us. But the songs remain
To search our wounds and bring us balm,
Till every song becomes a psalm,
And your restraint is our refrain;

Between the stained-glass and the stain,
The dark heart and the open vein,
Between the heart-storm and the harm,
Like David's psalm.

I see you by the windowpane,
Alive within your own domain,
The light is strong, the seas are calm,
You chant again the telling charm,
That names, and naming, heals our pain,
Like David's psalm.

Invitation

'I see you in the russet woods
And on the windy lea,
I hear the rhythm in your blood,
Now won't you dance with me?

Your heart is dark and overcast
And you can scarcely see
But grief would soon be overpast
If you would dance with me.'

'I cannot lift my weary feet
Or turn my heavy head
For I am clasped and spoken for
By one amongst the dead,

If I should turn, if I should hear
The voice that calls so free
I should betray the vanished love
Who waits beneath for me.'

'Oh she is gone away from you,
You may not follow now,
The night is cold, the door is closed,
You cannot keep your vow.

She cannot heed your crying now,
She cannot feel your pain,
Nor kiss the sorrow from your brow,
She will not come again.

The dance is for the living, love,
The dance is for the free
The dance is in our loving hearts,
Now won't you dance with me?'

Nothing Said

I wish that I could tell you, but I can't.
The sound sticks in my throat before I start.
You take an open question as a taunt,
I tell it whole, you take it all apart.
I wish that I could tell you, but I can't.

You wouldn't understand so what's the point?
You tell me 'there's the devil still to pay'
And I reply 'the times are out of joint',
We lurch between quotation and cliché.
You wouldn't understand so what's the point?

And so we waste our words with nothing said.
You keep your counsel close and I keep mine.
We take our turns with trivia instead
Twittering down a tedious decline
And so we waste our words, with nothing said.

Discomfited

Le coeur a ses raisons que la raison ne connaît point.
Pascal

Nothing can stay or comfort me
Not apples love, nor raisins
I grieve that nothing ever stays
Though all things have their seasons.

The luscious fruit of summer's love
Is scant and getting scanter
Just apples for the autumn now,
And raisins for the winter.

The heart must have its reasons, love
The reason never knows,
Some things die, and some survive,
Beneath its winter snows.

Since there's no stay or comfort through
The heart's severer seasons
Leave if you must my love, but leave
No crumbs for comfort when I grieve,
Leave me no raisins love, just leave,
I know you have your reasons.

Different Trains

It's not that we don't empathise,
Or hear each other's lonely sighs,
But this impediment remains:
We know we wait for different trains.

We feel the pang of hope deferred,
And tread the brink of the absurd,
As time runs out in tiny grains,
We know we wait for different trains.

We turn, we touch, we sigh, we weep,
We love the company we keep,
We part at last. No one complains;
We know we wait for different trains.

A Wealth of Images and Memories

A wealth of images and memories
Of hair and cross and breasts and giddy scents,
Of conversations, clichéd and intense,
In cluttered rooms and under root-fast trees
Where our exchange of breath-blown pleasantries
Rippled across a deepening innocence.

And if you leave, I leave, you leave me these
These leaves of memory so thickly falling,
Flame-coloured, floating slowly from the trees
Through dappled light and into shadows drifting,
Becoming earth, decaying by degrees
To loam-deep stillness we will keep at parting.

Whatever lies ahead you gave me these
A wealth of images and memories.

A Song Remembered

It was All Hallows, in the dying light
As leaves were falling, floating, frail and slow
I took the pathway between day and night
And heard the voice of one I used to know:

Who is it that this dark night
Underneath my window plaineth?

I heard her in the wind still keening, calling,
Keeping the echo of an idle song,
Far off I heard my answer, rising, falling,
Alone and lonely, longing to belong:

It is one who from thy sight
Being, ah, exil'd, disdaineth
Every other vulgar light

It was All Hallows, from the dying light
I turned, and at an altar lit my candle,
As though that gesture might keep back the night,
Or summon her again before my sight,
Or give me warmth again in my long vigil.
Alas I had no other light to kindle.

Out for the Count

i.m.
Neal Cassady

Tongue-tied as I count the rail-road ties,
The crucifying cross-beams of my dream,
You roll me on your scroll and count me in
With angel-headed hipsters, cowboy junkies,
A panoply freewheelin' thru' your head,
Count me with the ghosts, the countless shadows,
The hardly-living and the grateful dead.
Call me and count me, call me 'Cowboy Neal'
Call me The Dean my friend and count me in,
Make me another poetry projection,
And run my life out on your empty screen.
Co-opt me as the driver of your dreams,
Your drunken angel on the magic bus.
Count me in before you count me out,
Love me before you see me crucified,
Before the rain man gives me my two cures,
Tongue-tied, as I count the rail-road ties.

The Last Waltz

i.m.
Peter Boursnell

This poem should be PLAYED LOUD! 'Turn it up
A little higher on your radio'
And let me hear a song of love and hope
Made for the man who raised up all the low,
Lifted their gifts that they might aim still higher,
Who climbed his mountains too, and gave that power
To everyone he taught, helped them aspire,
The overlooked, to scale the ivory tower.

Turn up the volume, Pete, play *The Last Waltz*,
Strum out your life and say 'they've got it now',
Play the true note that blows away the false,
Take your deserved applause, your final bow.
You leave this stage but still your song is sung,
In grateful hearts you'll stay *Forever Young*.

Mistakes

I fought in the old revolution.
Leonard Cohen

When I turned teen in nineteen-sixty-nine
I heard of revolution in the air,
Well, on the air, in fact on 'Caroline'.
Lennon and Lenin had so much to share;
A change would come and change would be benign,
A fairer world, and all the world a fair!
'Here comes the sun' we sang to blissed-out skies
And thought the bomber jets were butterflies.

We conjured faeries out of every flower
But something wicked slipped out with the weed.
Stoned circles never yet spoke truth to power,
And groovers were grasped soon enough by greed.
For, after Altamonte, our world turned sour
And self-consuming souls turned onto speed.
The times were out of joint, oh cursed spite!
We thought just one more joint would set them right!

Since revolution's once more in the air
We'll learn from the mistakes we made back then;
We took a lot of everything but care
For we were just consumers in the end.
My counsel is no counsel of despair
It may not be too late to try again!
Our trips could never switch an institution
But just one crank can start a revolution.

Advice to a 'Statesman'

Bury the truth and lie down with a lie,
Dismiss the losers with a winning smile,
The dead are dead and cannot testify.

Hire a good brief to help you 'clarify'.
You've no regrets; regrets are not your style.
Bury the truth and lie down with a lie.

A few more headline grabs will get you by,
Always appear to go the extra mile,
The dead are dead and cannot testify.

Concede the odd 'mistake', contrive a sigh,
But wrap yourself in virtue all the while.
Bury the truth and lie down with a lie.

Most witnesses are dead, some you can buy,
Some can be lost in a 'deleted file',
The dead are dead and cannot testify.

The dreams may come, the screams that terrify...
They can be blocked with Prozac for a while.
Bury the truth, and lie down with a lie,

Until the dead arise and testify.

Distant

It's just those distant people we ignore,
Too indistinct for us, too far away,
But no one's really distant any more.

It's not that we are selfish to the core,
But life's too short to go out of your way,
It's just those distant people we ignore.

We're fine with people whom we've met before,
The ones with whom we're living day to day,
But no one's really distant any more.

They showed his little body on the shore,
A toddler who had drowned along the way,
One of those distant people we ignore,

One of the refugees, one of the poor,
And not so long ago or far away,
For no one's really distant anymore.

Who is this wounded stranger at my door,
Claiming to be the God I keep at bay,
And making claims on me I can't ignore,
Refusing to be distant anymore?

Observations

To stand in our doorway waiting for the sun,
Shrouded in murk, to set with exact stealth
On our shed, our cabbage patch, our hen-run,

Our just allotment of the commonwealth,
To hide us both with these things in the dark
Was once the solace of my youth and health.

Not anymore. I no longer remark
On these fenland sunsets as I used to,
To taxi drivers and to lovers in the park –

No. I am indoors now, writing to you
Out of idleness perhaps, not sentiment,
For now I hardly feel the things I do,

By lamplight in a different compartment
Placing my thoughts in line by threes
On blue paper provided by the Government.

I am a man impressed by what he sees.
From here you can see a vandalized phone-booth,
A monument, a clock, two stunted trees,

A frail pensioner and a violent youth.
God gave you a great riddle to solve,
He granted me this mediocre truth.

Empty

Outside an owl calls to the empty sky
As October prises him open
And drains each day into darkness.
He waits for these words at his window
And lamplight falls on the linked letters
Placed to no purpose on an open page.
Their land lies open also, exposed
In all its folds and fields to frost,
They feel its fingers write in the furrows.
Soon they will sleep, not side by side,
But each with another, each turned away,
Letting the letters unlock, that linked them.
They lie, like these letters, like the land around them,
Under a dark sky, open and empty.

Earth to Earth

We are what the land lends us,
Brief tenants
Of familiar haunts,
Owed back to all that owns us,

Old earth's articulated mud,
Humours becoming humus,
Her darkness drains through us
In rivers of good and bad blood.

Yellow and mottled grey and black and brown,
We carry her colours, drink from her cup,
The earth we think we own has made us up,
And she will break us down.

To Make an End

Now I begin to want to make an end
And to have done with everything. This long
Drawn-out bloody business of our kind:
This being where we clearly don't belong,
These beating hearts, the breathing, the repeating,
Repeating everything until our stop
Comes finally, and late, the breath abating,
The last gasp done, and we can drop.

Unless that end is only a beginning
And, as some say, the whole thing starts again:
The lonely losing and the weary winning,
But deeper in the mire, much further down.
Perhaps there's no way out, it's only how
You bear with it that matters, starting now.

November's Song

November sings its song with tongues of fire
From the first flame of candles for the dead
To the last embers of an old desire
Shifting to ashen grey from glowing red.

From the first flame of candles for the dead
A mass for All Souls held against the dark
Shifting to ashen grey from glowing red
Till dust and ashes smother every spark.

A mass for All Souls held against the dark
Kindles an old flame till it's bonfire night
Till dust and ashes smother every spark
And faces, strangely changed in firelight

Kindle old flames, until it's bonfire night.
Then comes the shadow of Remembrance Day,
For faces strangely changed in firelight
Are ashes now, or lowered in the clay.

Out of the shadow of Remembrance Day,
Out of the embers of an old desire,
Out of these ashes and this silent clay,
November sings its song with tongues of fire.

Remembrance Sunday Afternoon

November sunlight shimmers on the Wear,
Wide waters slip unhurried by each bank
And soothe Remembrance Sunday afternoon.
After the service, after the parades,
After the poppies, after the last post,
I sit and drink in quietness and peace,
The peace those Durham infantry forsook
To keep it sacred for the likes of me.
Some of them surely fished this very spot
Where Durham fishermen are sitting still
On folded campstools. May those fallen men
Whom we remembered in the high cathedral
Drink deep now from the river of true life
Where all their wounds are healed, where living light
Flows from the source of every time and tide
And may they know that we remember them.

Two Sonnets

For Ed and Wendy Peterson on their
Golden Wedding Anniversary

I

How many rivers merged, the day you met?
Your stories map the story of your nation;
Its tragedies and triumphs made you, yet
The Spirit made you new by true adoption.
One with the Son, you found the Faithful Father,
Who gave the gift of parenthood to you.
Where others scattered, you were called to gather,
Redeem the broken vows and make them true.

Red River's songs are running in your veins,
An ancient people yearn to be made new,
And now you speak for them, and take the pains
To open up their pathways, clear the view,
And grow the roots of true community,
That all your children's children might be free.

II

A golden anniversary! The fruitful grain
Shines sheer and clear, the chaff has blown away,
And you who sowed in tears, who sowed in pain,
Can reap with songs of joy, as on this day
You glimpse again the promises of love:
Your promises to love and Love's own promise:
I am with you always. When you grieve
My wounds will weep with you. When you rejoice
My joy will deepen yours. And you will be
With me forever, as I am with you
For all times – and with me all times are soon!
Keep trusting all your promises to me,
As long ago, you tried, and found me true,
One wild November day in Saskatoon.

The Great Physician

For Den Conneen, an Emergency Room doctor,
on his retirement

What grace emerges from emergency,
How many births spring from apparent death,
When reassurance calms our urgency
With prayer and skill, restoring life and breath.
You faced the traumas where our fears still lurk
And brought your patients back to home and health,
Their sudden crisis was your daily work
Yet so few knew, for you did good by stealth.

Now we stand back and look along those years:
Hundreds alive and breathing thanks to you!
But you did more than stem the blood and tears;
You sowed a harvest that you never knew
And gently led the patients you made whole
To meet the Great Physician of the soul.

Seven Poems from *Ordinary Saints*

1 Ordinary Saints

The ordinary saints, the ones we know,
Our too-familiar family and friends,
When shall we see them? Who can truly show
Whilst still rough-hewn, the God who shapes our ends?
Who will unveil the presence, glimpse the gold
That is and always was our common ground,
Stretch out a finger, feel, along the fold
To find the flaw, to touch and search that wound
From which the light we never noticed fell
Into our lives? Remember how we turned
To look at them, and they looked back? That full-
Eyed love unselved us, and we turned around,
Unready for the wrench and reach of grace.
But one day we will see them face to face.

2 A Portrait of the Artist

Ah, but we want so much more – something the books
on aesthetics take little notice of. But the poets and the
mythologies know all about it. We do not want merely to see
beauty, though, God knows, even that is bounty enough. We
want something else – which can hardly be put into words –
to be united with the beauty we see, to pass into it, to receive
it into ourselves, to bathe in it, to become part of it.
C. S. Lewis, *The Weight of Glory*

There is a presence and an absence here;
The artist sets himself aside, leaves space
For his shy muse. Descending from her sphere

She shimmers through his touch and brush, which place
These faint suggestions of her presence, where
She arches just behind him, full of grace.

He looks another way, as though aware
That turning round to see would frighten her.
He cannot see, we cannot help but stare,

Where light and shade, informing one another,
Call forth the forms that haunt his staring eyes;
Beauties from which not one of us recover.

Beauties of gold and green appear and rise
Behind him like the walls of the Duomo
Which hold the body and its mysteries,

For he has summoned them, like Prospero,
Spirits of air and fire, water, earth,
They haunt him now and will not let him go

Until he paints for them the secret path
Whereby they might grow visible at last,
Until he brings them to their proper birth.

And in their presence we are found and lost:
What finds us here is haunting, numinous,
And opens out the secret of our past

That longing, inconsolable, within us
For beauty, yes, and yet for something more,
Not just to see the lovely, luminous

Appearances of nature, but to pour
Ourselves into and through them, to receive
Them into us, till beauty, grace, and power

Become the very world in which we live,
The air we breathe, the light by which we see,
And we are one with all the things we love.

And what we lose is our complacency;
The daily comfort of the commonplace,
Our cherished substitutes for grace and glory.

These lines of longing in us somehow trace
A portrait of the Artist who has made us
And waits for us to turn and see his face.

3 A Shared Motif

A portrait of the Shaw Family

To be a person is to be a gift
Given in love. For each of us receive
The gift of being from another and we lift
Each other into light with every glance,
Given and returned in this long dance.
We have become ourselves through fathers, mothers,
All whose traces, and whose grace-notes, leave
Us all the more the people that we are.

Playing for others, in our turn, we hear
Our own tune, in a new key, played by others.
So with this family: each at their ease,
Relaxed within themselves, and yet aware
Of one another, as a simple grace
Sounds its soft motif through the quiet air.

4 A Portrait of Scott Cairns

We face a man who's been out to the edge.
All of us harrow Hell, but none can come
Through Paradise unscathed. From the high ledge
Of the holy mountain few come home
To bring us news, and help us share the burden:
Christ's beauty and his sorrow, meeting us
In every place and person, lest we harden
Our hearts to him, lest we avert our gaze

From God's iconostasis, flickering
In the strong faces of his ordinary saints
Lit by their little fires and beckoning
Us on with them to heaven. Cross-light slants
On to this picture of Christ's scathing grace:
A poet's burdened and unburdened face.

5 Portrait of the Artist's Father

Here is your father, looking out at us
From this dark room where shadows furl and fold,
Patiently present to whoever comes,
Still on his battered sofa, at his ease.
He looks out from the darkness of the world,
The copper blotch and mottle of old time
Whose tarnishes and patina reveal
Strange beauty in the saints we love and leave,
Whose leaving leaves us burnished as we grieve.
He meets us here, at home in his own skin,
Which holds more colours than the eye can trace,
More substance, more humanity and grace
Than paint on wood can possibly contain,
All in the clarity of his kind face.

6 Portrait of the Artist's Mother

Red over gold and under gold a wound
Whence life itself in blood and water flows,
A branch is broken but the tree still grows
The scar is over-layered with bark, a space
Which opens through the gold to blood-stained ground.
And now the wood itself presents her to us,
That wound above her opens out to us,
But cannot yet disclose its inwardness,
So she herself, beneath it, leaning out
And looking past us is still holding in,
The singing soul still shining through her skin.
A different darkness and a different light
Kindle her eyes, which hold us for a while,
And see more sorrow than there's time to tell.

7 Sitting for Bruce

Prepared

This flat wood, covered with its squares of gold
Through which my blurred reflection comes and goes
Will one day hold my image; it will hold
The face I cannot see up to the world.
For now, it keeps its secret, only shows
Across its bright gold-leaf some scars and flaws
And one thin streak of red, an open wound
From which I'm told my portrait will emerge.

Till then this waiting space will hold its charge;
The strong potential of its golden ground,
A light behind my back, before my mind,
A blaze beneath the sill of what I am,
That tells me I am always on the verge
Of something that I haven't yet become.

Abraded

Bruce Herman takes a sander to the gold
To shape my likeness in the clay and dust.
His hands are bleeding as he takes a hold
Of this abrasion, for he knows he must
Unmake the thing he's made to make it better.
He opens out and flays the gold and clay
Unveiling shapes and painting with the sander,
I see my face half-formed, and look away.

He takes me back to all that grinds me down
Strips my defences, leaving me exposed,
I flinch back from the form he has disclosed
As though I had been opened to the bone.
He is not finished. Now he paints through pain
The subtle strokes that make me whole again.

Finished

For I am incomplete, my mirrors show
No more than flaws and fragments as they pass,
The selves I lose, that mock me as they go
And leave me trembling by the darkened glass.
I do not see the face that once I had
Nor can I see the one I will become,
Flitting between a shadow and a shade
I was, I was, I whisper, not *I Am*.

And then comes One who calls me from my ruin
As from this bricolage of dust and stain
He works to build what I have broken down
Outfaces me, and finds my face again,
Just as this artist summons me to see
How grief and joy and time might finish me.

The Seasons' Benedictions

Spring

With each unfolding seed, with every spring,
He breathes the rumour of his resurrection,
As birdsong calls your hidden heart to sing.
So may this season be his benediction,
To lift your love, and bid your prayer take wing,
To thaw your frozen hope, to warm your mind,
For spring has come! Can heaven be far behind?

Summer

When young-leafed June is summoned by the sun,
And new-mown grass breathes fragrance through the air,
When work is over, holidays begun,
May peace and pleasure in themselves be prayer.
And in your leisure may you hear the one
Who is your blessing and by whom you're blest
Still calling you: *Come unto me and rest.*

Autumn

Now for the harvest! All is rich and full;
The swelling grape is ripe upon the vine,
So may his blessing sanctify your fall,
And old love be remembered in new wine.
Now may your ears be open to his call,
You stand on holy ground, look up and see:
His love burns red and gold in every tree.

Winter

When winter comes and winds are cold and keen,
When nights are darkest, though the stars shine bright,
When life shrinks to its roots, or sleeps unseen,
Then may he bless and bring you to his light.
For he has come at last, and can be seen,
God's love made vulnerable, tightly curled:
The Winter Child, The Saviour Of The World.